Sticker Grammar and Punctuation for School

Written by Jane West
Illustrated by Ian Cunliffe

Nouns

> **Hints and tips**
>
> - **Common nouns** are the names given to things or people.
>   blanket   car   dog
>
> - **Proper nouns** are the names given to people, places, days of the week and titles. Proper nouns always start with a capital letter.
>   August   Mum   Mr Spicer

Circle the nouns in the story below. Circle common nouns blue and circle proper nouns red.

Foxy goes to the vet

Foxy felt ill. He lay in his basket and wouldn't eat his breakfast. Jessie said, "Mum, Foxy is ill. What can we do to help him?" Jessie looked worried.

"I think we should take Foxy to the vet," said Mum. Jessie wrapped Foxy in his blanket. They drove to see Mr Spicer.

A noun is a word used to name a thing or feeling.

"Hmm," he said. "Foxy has a blocked nose, that's all. A dog only eats when he can smell his food. He'll be better soon." Soon Foxy was barking at the cat next door and was completely back to normal.

Read the story again. Write all of the common nouns below in the order that they appear. Can you find a sticker to match each one?

Singular and plural

Hints and tips

- **Singular** means one thing
  book   dish   fly
- **Plural** means two or more
  books   dishes   flies

  As you can see above, most plural words end with the letters s, es, or ies.

- Some plurals do not end with the letter **s**. We call these plurals irregular, for example,
  women   children   feet
- Some nouns have just one word for both singular and plural. For example,
  butter   sand   snow

Write the plural ending to each of the nouns below.

In my dream I saw…

One hen in her den.

Two cat_s_ chasing rat_s_ .

Three witch_es_ in soup dish_es_ .

Four bee_s_ buzzing in tree_s_ .

Five lad_dies_ with crying bab_ies_ .

Six goat_s_ in woolly coat_s_ .

Seven brother_s_ driving tractor_s_ .

Plural words show that there is more than one thing.

Find a sticker to go with each **plural** word.

Verbs

> **Hints and tips**
> - A verb is a doing word.
>   I run   You run   He runs   She runs   They run   We run
> - The ending of a verb changes depending on who is speaking.
>   Here are some other examples.
>   I kiss   You kiss   He kisses   She kisses   They kiss   We kiss
>   I try   You try   He tries   She tries   They try   We try

Which verbs do you think these pictures show? The first one is done for you.

read

Jump

Sleep

Swim

Complete the cartoon strip opposite by finding the stickers and writing the correct verbs in the spaces.

play   shouts   jump   says

6

A verb is a word which says what we are doing.

Football fun!

Sometimes I _like_ football with my big brother.

When I score, he _said_ "Goal!"

Then I _jump_ up and down because I'm happy.

'Well done!' He _said_ .

The end

Past, present and future

Hints and tips

- The present tense = something that is happening now

  I play basketball or I am playing basketball.

- The past tense = something that has already happened

  I played basketball or I was playing basketball.

- The future tense = something that hasn't happened yet

  I will play basketball or I am going to play basketball.

- Most verbs in the past tense end in 'ed' (like 'I played')
- Some 'irregular verbs' don't follow this pattern. Here are some irregular verbs:

Present tense	Past tense	Future tense
I am	I was	I will be
I think	I thought	I shall think
I come	I came	I am going to come
I cry	I cried	I shall cry

Write a postcard to your friend using the past tense. Tell them what you did on holiday.

Dear dad please can you play football with me when we get home.

Lots of love

Joshua Lee

To
Dad Lee
Pewsey
Wiltshire
SN9 6LL

Past, present and future tenses help us to understand when something happens.

Here is a postcard. Underline all the verbs in the past tense.

Dear Addie,
Yesterday I went to the beach with my mum and sister. We found some pretty shells and pebbles. Tina found a crab! Mum bought some postcards and gave this one to me. I wish you were here too!

Kirstie x

To
Addie Parker
8 Lower Street
Springwell
AA3 9TP

When you have read the postcard, find some stickers to decorate the front. Use the writing on the postcard to help you.

Adjectives

Hints and tips

- An adjective is a describing word and is used with a noun.
  Look at the adjectives in this sentence.

  The **small** dog chased the **stripy** cat up a **tall** tree.

- Here are some other examples.

  fat   short   leafy   spotty   tiny   brown   furry   green

TIP! Using adjectives can make stories more interesting to read. Try using different adjectives when you write.
nice: lovely, gorgeous, fantastic, beautiful
bad: awful, horrible, nasty, mean, dreadful

Find a picture sticker to match each of the following sentences:

This is a **spotty** dog.

This is a **greedy** dog.

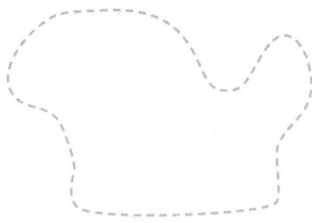

This is a **thin** dog.

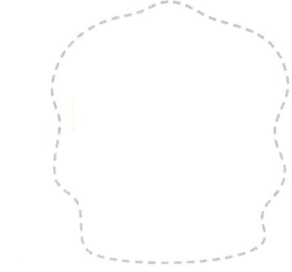

This is a **fat** dog.

An adjective is a word we use to describe the way something looks, feels, sounds or smells.

Find stickers to go with each of these words.

muddy muddier muddiest

hairy hairier hairiest

slow slower slowest

Adverbs

> **Hints and tips**
> - An adverb describes how or when something happens.
> - She ran upstairs quickly.
>   This adverb tells us how something happens.
> - I have football practice soon.
>   This adverb tells us when something happens.
> - It was too hot to play inside.
>   This adverb tells us where something happens.
> - The leopard runs really fast.
>   This adverb tells us by how much something happens.
> - I always have toast for breakfast.
>   This adverb tells us how often something happens.

Can you think of some sentences for these adverbs?

almost	I almost scored
quietly	I quietly sat down
now	Now we are going to the park.
often	I often watch tv.
beautifully	My bedroom was beautifully
outside	I went outside
never	I've never hated football
frequently	I frequently went to the library

Nouns – page 2

  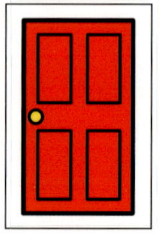

Singular and plural – page 4

Verbs – page 6

Adverbs – page 12

Conjunctions – page 14

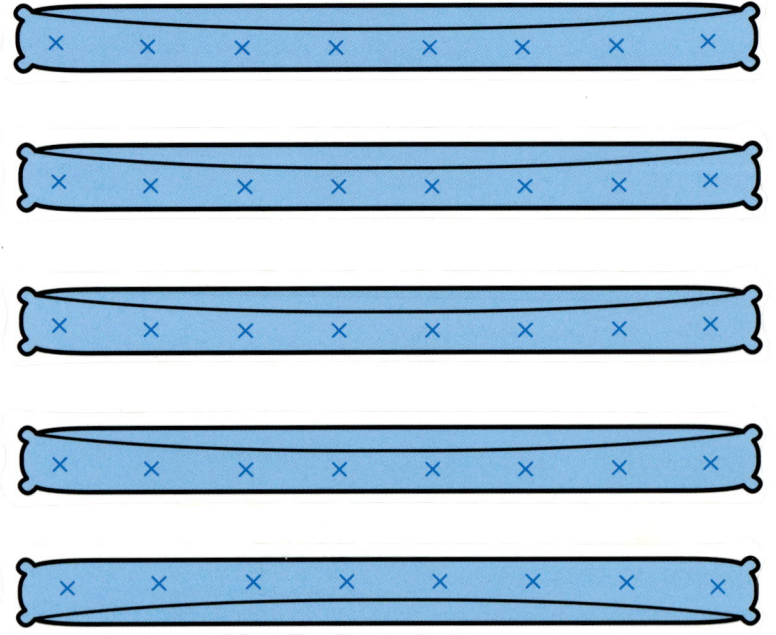
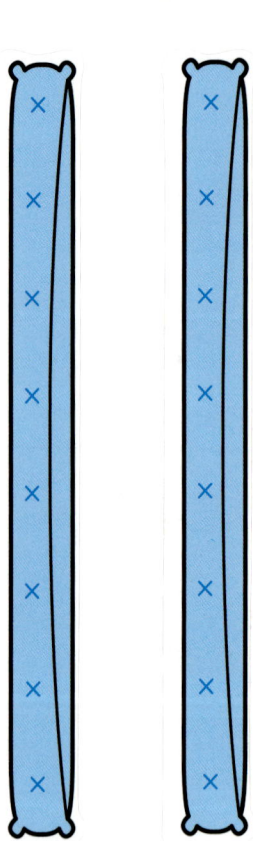

Sentences – page 16

| Put the second slice of bread on top. | Place some tuna and some cucumber on one slice of bread. |
| Cut the sandwich in half and eat. | Butter both slices of bread. |

Commas – page 18

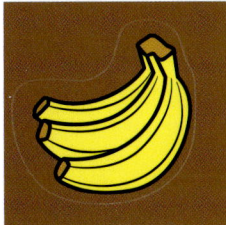     

Apostrophes – page 19

Reward – page 24

Past, present and future – page 9

Adjectives – page 10

An adverb gives extra meaning to a verb or sentence.

Find the missing picture stickers and complete the sentences about Foxy using one of the words below.

loudly ✓   really ✓✓   always ✓   quickly ✓   messily ✓

Foxy barks _really loudly_.

Foxy eats _messily_.

Foxy _always_ likes his walks.

Foxy is _really_ a good dog.

Conjunctions

Hints and tips

- A conjunction is a linking word. It links phrases or sentences together.
- Here are some common ones: **and but because so**

Read the story of the Princess and the Pea and underline each conjunction. The first one has been done for you.

The Princess and the Pea

There was once a Prince who wanted to find a wife, <u>but</u> however hard he looked, he could not find a single Princess that he wanted to marry.

One night there was a knock at the door, so the Prince and his mother the Queen went to see who it could be.

A girl stood in the doorway. "I am Princess Pandora. I was travelling to see my uncle, but I became lost in the fog." The Prince thought she was beautiful, so he invited her to stay.

The Queen said, "She is beautiful indeed, but is she a real Princess?" She took the girl upstairs.

In the bedchamber the girl found a bed piled high with mattresses.

A conjunction links sentences or phrases together.

The Princess climbed onto the top mattress, but however hard she tried, she could not sleep. The bed was too lumpy.

The next morning, the poor girl yawned at the breakfast table. The Queen was delighted. "Now I know that you are a real Princess, because only a princess would feel this tiny pea through all those mattresses."

Now count how many words you have underlined. Add a sticker mattress to the bed for each conjunction you have found.

Sentences

> **Hints and tips**
> - A sentence is a piece of writing that makes sense all by itself.
> - A sentence usually starts with a capital letter and ends with a full stop.
>
>   →There's a cup on the shelf.←
>   capital letter   full stop
>
> - If a question is being asked, a sentence ends with a question mark.
>
>   →Where is the cup?←
>   capital letter   question mark
>
> - To express a feeling, like surprise, some written sentences end with an exclamation mark.
>
>   →It's disappeared!←
>   capital letter   exclamation mark
>
> - A sentence always has a noun or a pronoun and a verb.

Add a full stop (.) question mark (?) or exclamation mark (!) to each of these sentences.

Charlie opened his birthday presents

That's amazing

How did you get inside without being seen

I live in Australia

Where do you live

You were brilliant

A sentence is a group of words which starts with a capital letter and ends with a full stop.

The pictures below are instructions for making a sandwich. Find a sticker sentence to match each one, so that the instructions make sense and are in the correct order.

Find two slices of wholemeal bread.

Commas

> **Hints and tips**
> - Commas can be used when you are writing a list.
> - Some sentences have commas to make them easier to read.
>
>   Although I like fish and chips, I prefer curry.
>
>   I ate sandwiches, salad, an apple and an orange.

Tom and Sam are playing the game, **I went to the market**. Read what each of them is saying and add commas in the right places. Find some sticker fruit to go in each basket.

I went to the market and I bought apples bananas plums a mango a pineapple and oranges.

I went to the market and I bought apples bananas plums a mango a pineapple oranges and a coconut.

Apostrophes

> **Hints and tips**
>
> - We use an apostrophe (') when we miss out one or more letters in a word.
>   **don't   we're   I'll   couldn't   o'clock**
>
> - We also use an apostrophe with the letter s to show that something belongs to someone or something.
>   **This is Ahmed's toy car.**

Whose books? Read each sentence and add the apostrophes, then find the missing book stickers.

It s a scary book belonging to Sally.

This is Jenny s story book.

I can t open this book.

My brother s book is about aeroplanes.

19

Speech marks

Hints and tips

- When we write, we show that someone is speaking by using speech marks (" ").
  "Come closer so that I can see you," said the wolf.
- A comma is used to separate the spoken words from the unspoken words, unless these end with a question mark or exclamation mark.

Read the story and write speech marks to make the sentences correct. The first one has been done for you.

Big Bad Pirate Bill

"Land ho!" yelled Pirate Bill.

Look at those lovely coconut trees,   shouted Pirate Pete.

Speech marks are the punctuation mark we use to show that someone is speaking.

Can't we land and play on the beach?   asked Pirate Penelope.

Well, just till two o'clock,   replied Bill. I'll just have forty winks.

Why didn't you wake me up?

Grammar and punctuation games

Here are some games that will help you to practise the grammar and punctuation you have learned in this book.

The adjective game

Think of a noun. What adjectives can you use to describe it? Think about the five senses (look, taste, feel, smell, touch) and try to paint a picture in your imagination.
For example: buttery, cool, creamy, tasty, icy, fruity, yellow ice cream!
Now try with 'dog', 'flower', 'cake', 'sand', 'photograph'.

What's one?

Here are some irregular plurals. Can you write down the singular noun?

wives _Wive_   women _Woman_   calves _calve_

children _children_   mice _mouse_   boxes _box_

switches _Switch_   potatoes _potatos_   heroes _hero_

people _person_   loaves _loave_   scarves _Scarve_

Twenty questions

Choose a famous person who your friends will know. They must ask you questions about the person until they can work out who it is. You can only answer them with "yes" or "no". If they don't guess who the person is in twenty questions then you are the winner.

Consequences

Practise writing sentences with this funny game. Write the first line of a story, then fold the paper over to cover your writing. Give the piece of paper to the next person and ask them to write the next line of the story. Keep handing the paper on until you come to the bottom of the page or finish the story, then read the story that you have written. Does it make sense?

Interview the wolf

If you could interview the wolf in **Little Red Riding Hood**, what would you ask? "Why are you so mean?", "Where are you from?" What might the wolf say in reply? Write a WANTED poster for the wolf using lots of adjectives. For example: mean, bad, wicked, nasty.